Post-Fondness

poems by

Michael O'Ryan

Finishing Line Press
Georgetown, Kentucky

Post-Fondness

Copyright © 2020 by Michael O'Ryan
ISBN 978-1-64662-208-5 First Edition
All rights reserved under International and Pan-American Copyright Conventions. No part of this book may be reproduced in any manner whatsoever without written permission from the publisher, except in the case of brief quotations embodied in critical articles and reviews.

ACKNOWLEDGMENTS

"Post-Fondness" originally appeared in *Tiniest Bit of Light* in an earlier version
"Poolside" originally appeared in *Cathexis Northwest Press*
"Embracing the Wind" originally appeared in *Five:2:One Magazine* under the title "Jude Sensed a Storm Coming"
"The Moral of the Story" originally appeared in *Oceans & Time* in an earlier version
"Autumn" originally appeared in *Five:2:One Magazine*
"Teenage" originally appeared in *Alien Mouth & Medium*
"Mad Dogs and Capricorns" originally appeared in *Pioneertown Literary Journal*

Publisher: Leah Maines
Editor: Christen Kincaid
Cover Art: Bill Livingstone/Shutterstock.com
Author Photo: Zoë Haakenstad
Cover Design: Michael O'Ryan

Printed in the USA on acid-free paper.
Order online: www.finishinglinepress.com
also available on amazon.com

Author inquiries and mail orders:
Finishing Line Press
P. O. Box 1626
Georgetown, Kentucky 40324
U. S. A.

Table of Contents

Post-Fondness 1

Fruit Rot 2

Poolside 3

This Sordid Dowry 4

Embracing the Wind 5

The Moral of the Story 6

Bodies 9

Autumn 10

Inheritances 11

Virginia 12

Porchlight 13

Milk 14

Teenage 15

Mad Dogs and Capricorns 16

Wildlife 17

sometimes paradise happens too early and leaves us shuddering in its wake

—Kaveh Akbar

Post-Fondness

Before:/ the swift catch-and-release of a
gaze from across the room/ noticing a slightly

darker shade of skin during the months
when the sun leaned into its season/

2 A.M., early summer and our splintering
innocence/ laughing until our heads fell off/

Now:/ a post-mortem profile picture is a modern-
day head in a glass jar/ our waking days

navigating this sci-fi/ saccharine immediacy/
glacé schemata collected from artificial lovers

like rogue oil derricks tilling toward slaked nirvana/
don't you miss the fields?/ don't you yearn

for dominion over something you could thieve
the life from?/ how fondly I look back on

the venetians lacerating melichrous light/
scattering your symmetries like a radar jammer.

Fruit Rot

I am thinking of how I
    cast myself into your
body of water as a votive,

        how much harder it should
    have been to swim in the
        apse of your stained light.

I am thinking of ribs, their
    fertility & how prone they
are to breakage. I am not new

        to life outside the garden—
    sanguine clouds hanging
        low like apples on a feeble

branch, valleys windless as
    bone. Lodestar—culprit of
my ardor, as strange as this

        may sound, I fear I
    am beginning to miss
        the smell of fruit rot.

Poolside

And there you are
just beneath the surface of the water
while I'm poolside saying

every moment divorced from grief is its own miracle

but the words bend through water
taking the form of what's convenient
for the medium they navigate
like the jagged shape a body assumes
when falling from a balcony
or the American definition of terrorism

consider peace as a portrait of the
untouched body—
docile as a field breathing,
virgin in all its parts
to the invasion of gracelessness

consider violence as a visual spectacle—
the way light ricochets off skin in heat
almost reduces brutality to a kind of
blooming shimmer

and yet—
I cannot seem to find the ecstasy in weightlessness
I need to feel the gravity—
to get crushed by the trauma
a thing inflicts upon the landscape
in order to call it by a name.

This Sordid Dowry

Do you remember walking through the trees
our skin shielded from the violence of barbarous
sunlight and then   the newfound breeze we
inherited when emerging from the boscage into an
open field acted as an exorcism   a marriage between
our bodies   and whatever feral truth should have
chosen to impose itself upon them   an axe
driving through phloem   wood soon to be
charred into light   therein lied a sordid dowry
consisting of the idea that a mystery's purpose
is what's exposed about those involved leading
up to its solving   O, Lord   Who killed Laura
Palmer?   O, Lord   The concept of no ultimate
oversight is   less terrifying   than the idea that we
might be held responsible for the dissonance
between what we think   and what we do instead.

Embracing the Wind

        The horizon's wicked atrophy;
drifting through fields as we   distill fragments
    from a countryside afternoon.
Mason jars overflow   with strawberry cadavers and
    lunar syrup.
        Winds crescendo toward lunacy while your eyes widen,
red rings splicing the green iris   burst into certain
    lucidity—
an emerald siege,   the rippling of scorched air just
    above a burning orchard.
        Occult riptides mine the valley for radio static—
Surf's up!   I hang loose in the barrel
        of a gun with radii
as equidistant from laceration   and paradise as a
    bird of prey holding flight.

The Moral of the Story

The initial
owners of
my childhood
dog had his
vocal tissue
removed
due to his
ceaseless
barking at
storms

in certain
cultures twins
were thought
to be the
cursed
harbingers
of floods
and quakes

imagine
your song
being ripped
from your
throat

imagine
existing as
both a
miracle and
your own
death rites
while
some people
move through
life sticking

their limbs in
animal traps
and playing in
traffic only
to come out
unscathed

in the original
story Pinocchio
throws hammers
at will and
lusts after
trees of gold
before being
wrung by
the neck

there's a lesson
somewhere
in there but
lately I've been
rejecting the
notion that
anything outside
of a body
expired is
subject to
object permanence
especially the
moral of
the story

you see the
concept of
grace is purely
contextual
the way a
predator's
stalking takes
the form of
a dance the
sound of a
forest burning
turns to
song and
so often
life becomes
a long
quiet
pleading
the slow
waking of a
giant from
slumber a
mute dog
watching
ribbons
of bright
lightning
split trees
into halves.

Bodies

Your body as a sling blade
my body as lush undergrowth

your body as once-verdant terra in extremis
my body as a farmer's prayer for rain

your body as a somnambulant gaze out the window at the Pacific Ocean
my body as a handgun on the coffee table

your body as phenomena in a rural community
my body as the primary source documents

your body as a Tuscan marionettist's deft string manipulation
my body as a yearning to navigate the world as a real boy

your body as a bucolic communal settlement
my body as the implausibility of human utopia

your body as a doomsday cult
my body as the Kool-Aid

your body as a snake preacher sedulously handling his instrument of God
my body as hemotoxin surging through a bloodstream

your body as my body, doused in waves and ceding from its
former self like the deliquescent calving of a glacier giving way to heat.

Autumn

There was a time in Eastern Europe
when men accused women of possessing
fluencies in the fervent barking of
three-legged dogs & supplying proxies
of black magic with nutrients from the
wellspring of the breast. Fools will
claim this fear of feminine power has
since waned with each passing harvest.

All apologies for whichever slurred
locution I dilate through the telephone line,
lulls piercing your supine murmur
feel like October surging through my veins.

Inheritances

even a house inherited is not a home   the family
graveyard   all of its ghosts   bareknuckle
fusillades   grandmother called you cursed   a whore
in a sundress   I cannot shoulder   these inheritances
what I can do   list my own: total disdain
for the sun   blue eyes that turn   like retching oceans
when caught by the light   a refusal to leave here
when I said   *look at the moon*   and you replied
                              but I cannot spend the night

Virginia

Suspended inanimately
in the purgatory
of the sun's
asymptotic slinking
toward the horizon,

existing in
aperture like
stray cats
between seasons,

I asked what
Virginia is like,
and you said

*it's a kind of soft,
rolling blue*

Porchlight

a name curdles   on the tongue
steady as a howl   blooming
through the nightscape   we prefer
to think all is still   until porchlight
lances the   thick murk   revealing
a column of flies   droning

Milk

When the doctor realized I was breech
        in the womb, they were forced to rip me
from it. How I envy the mechanic,

                the neurosurgeon—
        those striving to learn the inner workings
            of a thing. To understand my own body

seems impossible. The way you could tell me
        my autonomic functions abide by magic words
and dumb luck and I would have no counter

                to your positing. That I've grown numb to the
        fervency with which my blood rushes is a
            testament to the malleability of the self. I keep

bending until I break into these long nights
        in the wet, monomaniacally diving into the
heavy milk of moonlight. My first drink

                took place in an incubator, and to this day
        I continue to grow in the wrong direction
            like a flower drunk on gravity.

Teenage

Radical slow-jam cartography. Night-
    swimming in the wake of several broken

promises. This was a storm taking root
    in alluvial cognition. Snow-blind

fingertips navigating aspen bark stood no
    chance against the blizzard; gravitropism

is lost on havoc. The human brain
    is nature's obsolete supercomputer.

Mad Dogs and Capricorns

I often wonder what capacity canines hold
    for narcissism / I assume theirs is much lower than
ours / and that's ironic because much like a mad dog,
    some people are blind to their own charm under the misguidance
of instinct / life is like a twenty-four hour 7-11 the way only
    paying customers are allowed to loiter and there lies a lingering
threat of violence / life is like a grindhouse triple-feature
    the way we're all cloaked in an absence of light and no matter
how thorough the character development, the protagonist is always
    succeeded by a new one when the film fades to black / sometimes
our own development grows lithe with time / like when it was
    your hazel-eyed angel on the phone and you could nearly map
the distance in her voice while your heart splintered like
    faraway lightning / occasionally on some poorly-lit porch at night,
wayward strangers ask me what my sign is / they never know
    what to say when I tell them I'm a Capricorn / it's the terror
of the inherent uncertainty in the superfluid nature of the human
    psyche that draws people to a reliance on the orientation of astral
bodies to tell them who they are / the main difference between
    a person and a mad dog is the ability to mask rabidity once let off
the leash / I guess I'm disheartened by the fact that even a tame dog's
    horoscope cannot predict under which moon it will bear its teeth.

Wildlife

I keep the light on when I leave my room
to alleviate the burden of vacant space

mankind is bespoken as the razer of wildlife in
Bambi without once appearing on screen

a rodeo clown hesitates briefly in requiem before
shooting a broken-legged bull between the eyes

Dr. Jekyll is an allegory for the world because
he fell victim to his own creations in his sleep

you point your finger like a gun at a clique of fawns
dashing through a woodland glade and then you stop

*M*ichael is a writer from Denver, Colorado. He currently lives in the Pacific Northwest, where he earned a degree in Cinema Studies at the University of Oregon. His work has appeared in *Ghost City Review, Pioneertown Literary Journal, Five:2:One Magazine, Peach Mag, Medium* & elsewhere. Follow him on Twitter @m_oryan00 and Instagram @mike_no_lyin

www.ingramcontent.com/pod-product-compliance
Lightning Source LLC
LaVergne TN
LVHW041525070426
835507LV00013B/1831